MW01201300

Long-form Improvisation
&
the Art of Zen

A Manual for Advanced Performers

Jason Chin

iUniverse, Inc.
New York   Bloomington

Long-form Improvisation & the Art of Zen
A Manual for Advanced Performers

iUniverse books may be ordered through booksellers or by contacting:

iUniverse
1663 Liberty Drive
Bloomington, IN 47403
www.iuniverse.com
1-800-Authors (1-800-288-4677)

ISBN: 978-0-595-47198-0 (pbk)
ISBN: 978-0-595-91478-4 (ebk)

Printed in the United States of America

iUniverse rev. date: 2/05/09

Introduction

This book assumes that you have had some experience with long-form improvisation; either in class or on the stage. This first part of this book is technical and is meant for people with some improvisational experience, while the second part is designed for the experienced performer. Just as in any other discipline or skill there are compulsories that must be met before a performer should start out on their own (like ice skating, kung fu, or even simple English 101) and that's how it's divided. My goal here is to set a common, logical template for us to base our work on and then in the second half to explore the philosophical approach to improvisation. Hopefully, any questions raised in one-half can be answered in the other.

I've been teaching, performing and directing long-form improvisation for the past fifteen years and in that time I've watched the art form grow and evolve. The biggest influence in my life and work has been Del Close. Del was my teacher and we worked together at Chicago's iO Theater. He always stressed that improvisation was in itself a theatrical medium and should be treated as such. From teaching and directing I have observed certain ideas and practices that make the creation of realistic, and often hilarious, characters and scenes. My own personal quest to become a better performer has dovetailed with my quest to just become a better person. My explorations with Zen philosophy and technique were beginning to influence my own work onstage and in classrooms so I have decided to put them all together on paper. Much to my parents disappointment, I have decided to devote an inordinate amount of time to two studies in which there can be no true quantification or qualification. Consider this book then, as a sharing of experience and notes.

I believe in long-form improvisation as an art form. I look forward to the day that its disciplines and skills are taught and reinforced in colleges as widely as poetry and dance. I will be there on opening day for the first Equity-production of a long-form improv show. It's not that too far off. The very fact that you're reading this is a small step in that direction.

ZEN & THE ART

When people speak of a "moment of Zen" they're referring to a moment of effortless effort; when someone instantly knows what to do and how to do it. When everything else in the world falls away except for the exact task at hand, this enables humans to do great and wonderful things. Improvisers should strive for this effortless effort. To be completely in the moment, relating specifically to the other person on stage at that time, this is the highest goal. When everything else (the audience, "having" to be "funny", your day at your office job, the lighting, the stage) becomes a secondary concern next to the person standing on stage next to you, when you are completely and totally in that world...   ... that is your moment of Zen.

To know and to act are one and the same
- Samurai maxim

It is said that "zen" cannot be taught. I believe that one can open a "door" in your mind and that will create situations and cause events to appear that otherwise would not. Improvising a scene and fully, completely, totally committing to it; being so completely in the moment that you can almost predict the future of everything stage is a feeling that I wish every improviser could experience. Though I have been improvising for years, I can only recall about three times where I was "zen-like" in my performance. It's something to strive for and with the thoughts and exercises I have listed I hope to make the path a little easier for those following.

"...and now, A Brief History of Improv Time:"

The eighties and early nineties saw explosive growth in the popularity of improvisation in Chicago, Illinois. There, the Second City theater had (and still does) been using scenic improvisation for the creation of scripted comedy shows. Since its founding in 1959, Second City invited audiences to stay for free to watch the improvised scenes (and refining thereof) and some short-form improv games after the scripted sketch show. A training center was created to help educate actors and others who wished to learn the Second City style of improvisation, while the rest of the country primarily relied on the books Improvisation for the Theatre by Viola Spolin and Impro by Keith Johnstone.

There were brilliant teachers at the Second City and they helped to create an entire generation of performers who were able to do entire scenes based solely on a word or two from the audience.
One of the earliest members of the Second City was Del Close, who upon leaving Chicago, traveled to San Francisco during which time he experimented with a longer form of improv than just scenes and games and began work on what would eventually become known as The Harold.

When Close returned to Chicago, he directed more Second City shows, became "House Metaphysician" to Saturday Night Live, created the format for SCTV, and eventually left Second City again. The reasons for this departure were both philosophical and pharmaceutical. Close's dependence on narcotics and his growing belief that long-form improvisation was the end and not just the means to one, brought him to the then small, nomadic business called ImprovOlympic, run by improv doyenne Charna Halpern.

At Close's behest, ImprovOlympic dropped the short-form games they were using for their shows and began intensive training under his tutelage. In a few months, they began performing the long-form structure that Close began developing in San Francisco, The Harold. Close lived to see his dream of all long-form improvisational shows as the ImprovOlympic (now called the "iO") opened its own theater building in 1994. Close passed away in 1999.   Incredible advances in performing and instruction have occurring in the Windy City at great theaters like The Annoyance Theater, the Playground Co-op, The Second City, and other wonderful places where improvisation thrives.

State of the Art

As you read this there are several thousand people studying and performing improvisation in Chicago alone. There are dozens of shows opening and closing each and every week with varying degrees of success and ambition.   The explosion of improvisation hasn't necessarily translated to better shows, just more of them. Just as the explosion and prevalence of home video equipment did not result in better movies, both have created more amateur shows for friends and family to endure.   The idea that "anyone can improvise" is a fine concept, but a misleading one. Sure, any one can, but should they? Anyone can put out a fire, but who do you call when your home is aflame; the guy who took a few classes in water bucket-throwing or the professional fireman? There are too many improv shows across the nation with little or no regard to presentation, direction, or artistry and too much "anything-for-a-laugh" mentality. This book is designed to help those who wish to see improvisation grow as an artform; to evolve from its comedic roots and take its place as a marketable, repeatable, theatrical experience.

I have been performing, teaching, coaching and directing long-form improvisation for the more than a decade and while I've seen great strides in the presentation, feel and regard for long-form improvisation, I've also seen it get more and more watered down. It's almost like Hollywood's obsession with the summer blockbuster; more bang and flashier effects but little regard for characters and creativity. For every great two person show that demonstrates the glory and wonder of an unscripted show, there's a ten person show in the back of a bar denigrating the idea of long-form improvisation.   I realize that a great deal of what is in these pages will seem adversarial, but it comes from a place of love for the art and a desire to see it evolve and mature.   First, let us start with a simple philosophy; long-form improvisation is an art form.   Long-form improvisation is an attempt to create either a performance art theatrical piece or a one act play. Typically, one suggestion is taken and the piece lasts for an hour or more. Long-form improvisation's ultimate goal should be theatre without a script.   Short-form, or "game" improv (such as ComedySportz, TheaterSports, Whose Line Is It Anyway?) is not an art; it is a craft. Surely an honorable one, with many very talented people dedicated to it, but it is most certainly not an art.   While the art of improvisation has most definitely grown in acceptance and popularity it has a tendency to backslide into farce or simple scenic games.

Our most common frame of comedic reference, whether we like it or not, is the situation comedy. Most beginning long-form improvisation subconsciously follows the basic tenets of a 30 minute sit-com; set-up scene, dilemma, resolution scene. This is fine if all we intend to do is an improvised sit-com. Hopefully, and Del willing, we're striving for something more. We need to break out of the scenic constraints of the sit-com as well (i.e.: always edit on a laugh, outrageous declarations and entrances, improbable coincidences and misunderstandings.) Much of this sit-com paradigm relies on characters not knowing something vital; be it a misunderstood communication or a willful ignorance. This "dumbing-down" is particularly detrimental to improvisational work. The old improv axiom of "playing to the top of your intelligence" should extend to the character's intelligence as well. Playing willfully ignorant is, well, dumb.   These subconscious rules are holding long-form back from what it truly can, and should, be. For long-form improvisation to thrive and survive it needs to evolve beyond bars and games. It needs to outgrow being the Court Jester and allow itself to be taken seriously in the theatrical world as another medium for performance. Being an improviser should mean as much as being a dancer, a poet, an author; because being an improviser means you are all those things.

Technical knowledge is not enough. One must transcend techniques so that the art becomes an artless art, growing out of the unconscious.
- Daisetsu Suzuki

SCENES

The heart of any theatrical piece, much less long-form improvisation, is the scene. If you can't do a scene, then you shouldn't be on stage improvising and no matter what wonderful and creative form you've created, if it obfuscates the scene work (instead of enlightening and highlighting it) then you're doing your group a disservice. The same goes for many "high-tech" attempts at improv—no matter how many cameras, plasma screens or Pro Tools you ladle on, the performers must be able to do a scene.

Let us concentrate on the art of the scene. A scene is about the people onstage and their relationship with each other. That's it. Sounds pretty easy, doesn't it? Whatever the suggestion, whatever the setting, the scene must be about the people onstage and how those things affect their relationship. No matter how banal an opening line (often called an "initiation") is, it can be reacted to with emotion. And that line can be reacted to as well with emotion. When the players are using emotion vs. (or with) emotion, it will usually be good scene.

A scene is never about the suggestion, event or object; the scene is about how the people onstage are affected by those things. Del Close used to say that an improviser is a bit paranoid on-stage; every little thing, a toss-away comment, how someone opens a jar of pickles, does or not buy a newspaper means something deep and personal to the person observing it. How someone over (or under) reacts to startling news is something that can be reacted to with emotion for an improviser.

As mentioned before, one of the goals for long-form improvisation is to avoid the common traps of the television sit-com. On most sit-coms dramatic or outrageous declarations are followed up with a wisecrack or a commercial. This style of comedy has infiltrated our improvisation and many improv scenes rely on it. For more effective, emotional and ultimately better improvisation we must stop using these as crutches.

Let us see an emotional response to outrageous statements. "I'm sleeping with your boss." "I killed the dog" "I'm gay" are common surprise declarations that usually provoke a laugh of surprise and an edit. Wouldn't it be more fun, more interesting, and more challenging to the performers, if we were to follow up on that line? Let us see the reaction from the scene partner and allow the situation to affect the emotional relationship between the two people. Now, we don't want our scenes to become melodrama (and they will the first few times you attempt this) but we do want to see honest emotion on stage. An improviser can do great scenes if s/he installs the following Improv Scene Prime Directives and applies them:

Who is this person in the scene with me?

What are they really saying or doing?

How does that make me feel?

I will now reply and act.

Let's examine those Prime Directives one-at-a-time:

Who is the person in the scene with me? This can be easily answered. If you are the initiating party, then you probably have a good idea of who they and you are. If they have spoken first, then it's up to you to decide who they are. The more interesting your choice is, the better (be honest, how many scenes have you seen with boss/employee, parent/offspring, siblings, roommates? Surely there are more relationships for us to play with than those. Your decision should be internal, but obvious to your scene partner. Your choice should be logical and interesting.

Let's take a look at a rather bland opening line: "Honey, you forgot to throw out the garbage again." Who would be saying this to you? A spouse, a roommate, a parent, a teacher? Who? You get to decide. And that's part of the fun of improvisation—unless specifically stated, the scene partner can be anyone you want. The line above is pretty open to interpretation. A slight change (say, "Dearest Husband, you forgot to throw out the garbage again.") alters the entire scene and gives you plenty of information.

What are they really saying or doing?

By looking beyond what someone says or does and inferring what they truly mean we can better formulate an emotional response. If you've ever been in one of those heated, shouting matches with a boyfriend or girlfriend you know that there's no such thing as a throw-away line, everything said really means something else. The people we play on-stage (and they should be people, in that they are people who care about certain things and have a past, present and future.. we just happen to be visiting them in the present.)   "Honey, you forgot to throw out the garbage again." How do you interpret that sentence? Is it an accusation? A friendly reminder? Is it the first time your partner has said this to you since you've moved in? Is it the "billionth" time s/he has told you over the course of a 50-year marriage? Of course, some clue to the improvisers intent can be gleaned from, not only how they say it, but how they were physically posed when they said it. The fun of it is interpreting and then deciding how you "read" their initiation.

How does that make me feel?

The easiest one of these questions to answer. Based on whom is speaking to you (the answer to Question 1) and what they are really saying (the answer to Question 2) this should be fairly easy to figure out. Decide on an emotion to play and go with it. I will now reply and act.   "Honey, you forgot to throw out the garbage again."

Answer 1: my new husband, Answer 2: He's being a nag. Answer 3: Annoyed, Reply: "Why don't you tell me again, Pete? I didn't hear you the first 20 times."

Answer 1: my wife of 30 years, Answer 2: She's actually reminding me of something else, Answer 3: loving, Reply: "You minx, you know that turns me on."

Answer 1: my roommate, Answer 2: He is coming on to me, Answer 3: confusion, Reply: "Dude, I told you not to call me honey. Quit it!"

If you follow these simple rules, you will have an easy time of creating personable, two-person relationship scenes.

If you cannot find the truth right where you are, where else do you expect to find it?
- Dogen Zenji

INITIATING A SCENE

There is nothing more frustrating than watching two improvisers enter a scene and then stand there looking at each other. There should be a purpose to each and every scene. Even if it starts with something banal or seemingly trivial, at least it has started. The question is the same one that has plagued writers, artists, and stand-up comedians for centuries; "Where do you get your ideas?"

Long-form improvisation should have a theme, an overriding motif. By referring to and discovering this theme, we should always be infused with ideas for new scenes. If a particular style or form becomes inhibiting to creating new scenes, then that style or form should be abandoned. If your ensemble gets a theme suggestion or not, there are easy ways to initiate scenes. We want to give some basic information, but not exposition. Let's not start with a scene idea, with but a line of dialogue or an action. We can proceed from there. From the audience's point of view it should feel like the scene was already in progress and they're getting a peek at it now. The people (not the characters, the people being portrayed) have lives that extend beyond what the audience can see and these lives influence how they feel and react to any given stimuli.

Suggestion example: Chinese New Year

Initiation examples: "Well, here we are in Chinatown!" – this overused trope of improv gives us nothing. It's not something that a real person would ever say.. it's more like something a narrator might say. It does nothing to help establish a relationship or situation, just a setting.

"Wow, this has been some year, hasn't it, John? I never thought that my own brother would be elected President of China and appoint me Minister of Defense!" – a classic example of overcomplicating, not only a scene, but an opening line. Take it easy there, Tex, it's too much at one time. The first sentence would have been fine... besides we really want the scene to be about the two of you and not the hilarious inner workings of the Chinese politburo.

"Happy Chinese New Year!" – while this seems perfectly fine, it does nothing for us. Also, it hits the mark a bit too close... we want to explore further a field from the initial suggestion.. we want to see themes and ideas that stem from the suggestion. That's not to say that this might not happen eventually in a scene that begins with this line, but let's see what we can do to better our chances of beginning a scene more effectively.

Still using the suggestion of "Chinese New Year" let's take a look at some other initiations:

"Mm. This chicken is great. Thanks for ordering, Jeff." – This seemingly ordinary initiation tells us a great deal. As audience members we can firmly see where it comes from and as an improviser it tells me that it's a fairly casual affair, probably just two friends hanging out over some take-out. Jeff is probably the more organized of the two people on stage.

"I am so jealous; I really wish I spoke two languages like you." – What a great gift to give a fellow performer- they can now speak two languages and the line also gives us information about the person saying it. The scene can use both of those tidbits to great effect simply by following the emotional clues.

"Happy American New Year!" – this could be just a joke unless we follow up and actually do an entire scene exploring how other countries might see our holiday traditions.

This style of initiation is more conducive to creating relationships with engaging people/characters than an initiation that is solely a comedic premise.

With longer, more advanced long-form improvisation there are two schools of thought on how to start a scene; hard and soft. A hard initiation starts with a definitive opening line that the improviser is saying for a particular reason. If you examine some of the forms discussed in this book you'll see that some scenes are designed to explore a theme or motif and thus scenes need to begin with a specific idea.

A soft initiation is a bit slower and allows for both players to "discover" the scene together. Both enter without any preconceived notions and build the scene one line at a time. Neither is better than the other in a general sense, but if the group consensus is to explore a suggestion thematically, perhaps hard initiations are more warranted. If a smaller group just wishes to explore characters and scenes, then perhaps soft initiations are the way to go.

Creating a Past

Even though we are creating entirely new characters on the spot, it's so much stronger to have these characters all know each other and have a shared past. The characters on stage have known each other for days, months, years which makes each emotional shift have greater resonance. But how to establish a past without dwelling on it? How to establish a shared world? If, as a player, we assume a shared past, the characters should behave the same way. A good way to establish a relationship is simply by adding a name, term of endearment, or even an honorific after a line (of course, the earlier the better). "There's your breakfast." would become "There's your breakfast, Harry." or "There's your breakfast, my beloved." or even, "There's your breakfast, Your Majesty." In most cases, scenes depict something new to the relationship. Something externally (the environment, time, etc.) has prompted an internal (feelings, philosophy, etc.) change in one of the characters that will be revealed in this scene. "I just had a roast beef sandwich" is a pretty banal line unless it's uttered by someone you know is a vegetarian. As previously discussed, the two-person scene is the heart of every long-form improvisation. There is a tendency to forget this and allow the format of a show dictate the scene work. This is a mistake. Roger Ebert says, "A movie is not about what it is about. It is about how it is about it." I say: It's not about the situation; it's how that situation affects not only the characters, but the relationship between the two.

I'm about to shock you with some tips on two-person scene work-Conflict is good. Argument is good.

A heated emotional exchange between two people is interesting if they're being led by their hearts. An argument between lovers, siblings, co-workers, is interesting if the people involved are being affected emotionally by everything said and done. A debate, on the other hand, is deadly. A debate is simply the presentation of facts determined to sway your opponent to your point of view. A debate between two people on the facts of scene is boring and tedious; and again, a heated emotional exchange will lead to interesting scene work.

It's Never Just Business.

In the Godfather movie, Michael Coreleone dispassionately discusses his assassination of Sollozzo and the police captain, McClusky. "It's not personal," he says, "It's business." The novel, however, goes one step further: "Tom, don't let anyone kid you. It's all personal, every bit of business. Every piece of shit every man has to eat every day of his life is personal. They call it business. OK. But it's personal as hell. You know where I learned that from? The Don. My old man. The Godfather. If a bolt of lightning hit a friend of his - the old man would take it personal. He took my going into the Marines personal. That's what makes him great. The Great Don. He takes everything personal."

And that's what we're looking for here. To take and to make everything personal. Not everyone can, or even should be, related to each other in a scene, but creating that personal, emotional connection will enable the scene to go further than just 1, 2 ,3 and scene. Make it personal. Take it personally.

Declarations of Co-dependence

As an improviser we never really get a chance to sit down with the director or playwright and ask what a characters motivation is for a particular scene. We don't get to parse each inflection and word for hidden meanings or feelings. We have to do it on the fly.   Improv is probably the only medium where an actor can get away with simply declaring their feelings at almost any given moment. Bluntly announcing your love (or hate) for someone during a scene in movie might seem clunky, but in improv it's both necessary and right.

THE GAME OF THE SCENE

Recognizing and/or creating a "game" within a scene is something that is very important to creating comedic improvisation. Knowing the next step in a pattern, setting up the next step, all of that is important to playing the "game" in comedic improv. The 1-2-3, cha-cha-cha pattern of improv is based on the creation of a joke; premise, set-up, punch line. For a visual representation of that kind of structure take a look at any comic strip in a newspaper. There's establishing panels, a set-up, and then the last panel has the punch line. There is a subtle science to comedy that encourages pattern building and repetition. Knowing how to recognize and heighten a pattern is a good skill for an improviser to have, but "playing the game of a scene" is often counter-productive to creating meaningful long-form improvisation. "Playing a game" makes a performer think about the next move instead of feel about the relationship. A "game" implies rules and an end result; these things are counter to what we should strive for with our improvisation. A well established game has a definable pattern that an audience can follow and sometimes predict the ending and, especially in improv, what fun is that? Without a "game" can long-form improvisation be funny? Of course it can. Improvisation that slavishly follows the "game" of a scene is like old vaudeville; it's still comedy and will make an audience laugh, but the art has grown past that. Improvisation shouldn't attempt to ape other comedic styling by offering the same old "set-up / punch line" structure, but should instead offer smart, relationship-based scene work with a theme. It has a name, this kind of work; "theatre."

SCENEWORK SUMMARIZED

A scene begins as soon as at least one person has entered.   The first person either verbally or physically initiates the scene.   The second person has an emotional, personal reaction to the initiation.   The first person has an emotional, personal reaction to the second person.   Yeah. It's that simple.   Some tips: When people know each other or have some sort a shared back-story/history, it makes the scene much more interesting by raising the stakes for the two. If a stranger told you to go to hell, it may not affect you. If your lover or your child told you to go to hell, it's going to be a much more interesting scene.   Know where you are and use the environment of that room to flesh out your relationship. A break-up scene is going to play differently depending on whose house it is set in.   Don't dwell on extraneous things; how you feel right now is of the utmost importance.   Tell your scene partner how you feel straight out. "You make me so angry!" "That makes me very sad." Are all perfectly valid declarations for an improvised scene.   Add a comma. "Here's your sandwich COMMA honey/your majesty/Mrs. President." That comma will help.

Knowing others is wisdom; knowing yourself is Enlightenment.
- Lao-Tzu

CREATING / DISCOVERING A THEME

Like any great art form, improvisation requires a theme or motif to elevate it beyond its state of stage grace. An abstract painting isn't just a collection of pigments on a canvas; it means something more to the viewer. Any experienced group of improvisers can do an interesting and funny montage of scenes. It is a group of improvising artists that discover, nurture and explore a theme.   What is a theme though? I'm going to mash together some of the literal definitions of the word to come up with this: a recurrent element in an artistic work that is repeated or evoked in various parts of the composition. A theme is what a long-form piece is "really" about... instead of being just a mish-mosh of scenes, the overall piece is trying to say something about either the suggestion or the theme that was prompted from the suggestion. A show based on the suggestion of "candy" shouldn't be 50 minutes of candy-based scenes, but an exploration of what that word evokes (childhood, reward, etc.)

A poet or novelist would be forever paralyzed with indecision and hesitation if they had to contemplate what each word and phrase "really" meant... they do their best to create their piece and later, they (or other people) assign meaning to the piece by analyzing it. That's how our shows should be. Based on any given suggestion or opening, we can divine and explore different over-riding themes and motifs.   How does a group "get" a theme for their performance? Asking for a theme seems too heavy-handed and obvious. Let's look at some interesting ways to get a theme for performance.

Sheer Poetry

Ask for a line of poetry. Depending on your audience, this may be problematic. Most people do not have a line of poetry ready to fall trippingly from their tongue. The reward for using this method of suggestion/theme getting is twofold; it really lets your audience know where your group is coming from, that you're about to do something serious and meaningful. Secondly, poetry is open to interpretation. For example: "I took the path less traveled and that has made all the difference." (You remember that from your Norton Anthology, don't you?) This opens up all possibilities for improvisational exploration; we can do scenes based on the literal statement (travel, camping, being lost and or found) or the figurative (dramatic choices, life regrets, the difference one moment makes in your life). Alternating between these two types of scenes is an enjoyable process as well.

Who Listens to Lyrics Anymore?   Asking for a lyric from a song requires more work from you and your group than poetry. Most of the lyrics that stick in peoples mind are silly. The trick here is to not act out the lyrics, but to interpret them; what is this song/lyric really about? As in the case with "Baby, Hit Me One More Time", the song is about a force of love so powerful that it feels like a physical hit (I know, we're perhaps giving the writer and songstress too much credit here). Now, that's a theme. That's a wonderful concept to play with. As with much of long-form improvisation, a useful tool is the question, "What is this really about?"

Art for Art's Sake   I have known groups who have had the audience choose a song from a collection of provided CDs, choose a painting from an art book, or even had the audience create their own painting before the show. Again, the trick behind any of these is to look beyond what is being said verbally and examine what is meant. These are all great ideas and help to reinforce the notion that long-form improvisation is an art form.

Word Pattern   This is probably the most popular type of "opening" for long-form improvisation. Using a single suggestion as a launch point, a group of improvisers play word association, riffing off each other until a climatic ending (either by coming back to original word or a major theme of the pattern.) A good way to look at this is that the group is creating a word-at-a-time poem based on an audience suggestion. After the "poem" is created, we can examine what it's really about. For example: Childhood as a suggestion leads us to create the following pattern: kicking and screaming, soccer, play ball, cooperation, sharing, buffet, Las Vegas, gambling, marriage, pregnant, childhood. Now, what is this "poem" about (besides Childhood)? Competition (soccer, gambling), unions (cooperation, sharing, marriage, fertilization), great fodder for thematic work. Besides the literal to explore, we now have two abstract, human concepts to explore.

The trick in doing a word pattern effectively is to avoid pop culture references and jokes. A pop culture reference tends to bog down the poem into a self-referential pattern and prevents us from creating as deep a pattern as possible. The same holds true for jokes; they serve no purpose but to get a cheap laugh smack-dab in the middle of a poem. This is no good. (ex: "Childhood, kicking and screaming, Will Ferrel, Saturday Night Live, Bill Murray…" you see how fast a good poem can be derailed? What kind of scenes could we do based on this? Not very good ones.)   We shouldn't be overly concerned, on-stage, with a theme for our piece. It's a subconscious, hidden thing during the show that can be seen by those willing to look for it. It is within a piece that is being taken seriously (that is, the scenes have integrity and honesty) by the players and the audience that a theme and motif can be discovered. As stated earlier, these shows/forms deserve/demand a longer showcase for their explorations. Forty-five to sixty minutes are the usual spans of time for shows of this magnitude. This is, not coincidentally, the average length of most one-act plays.

SUGGESTIONS

Teaching or coaching long-form improvisation is tough. To be an audience of one is not easy and, if you do it long enough, sometimes it hard to come up with suggestions that will be effective and educational. A class/rehearsal suggestion should be both abstract and specific and allow the group to create from the suggestion, as opposed to react to the suggestion. The following list of suggestions have been field and classroom tested for maximum efficacy.

Winter, Life, Thanksgiving, America, Space, War, Science, Ocean, Fourth of July, History, Halloween, Mother, God, Industry, Funeral, Baby, Love, School, Telephone, Internet, Marriage, Diamond

Those are just a few suggested suggestions. Of course, the less the scenes have to do directly with the suggestion, the better.   That is to say, based on the suggestion of "Science" we wouldn't want to see five scenes in a row about scientists, rather we want to extrapolate from the suggestion and perhaps see scenes about people affected by science, a scene about religion, a scene about experimentation, a scene about faith, and then maybe a scene about scientists.

Empty your mind, be formless. Shapeless, like water. If you put water into a cup, it becomes the cup. You put water into a bottle and it becomes the bottle. You put it in a teapot it becomes the teapot. Now, water can flow or it can crash. Be water my friend.
-Bruce Lee

HOW TO REHEARSE A LONG-FORM SHOW

You must have a director that is not a cast member. Take turns, have an election, however you choose, it's imperative that this outside eye not be prejudiced or blinded by being a participant instead of an observer. This person's duty will be to observe the rehearsal and provide constructive criticism on the moves and scene work.

Try doing a form for thirty minutes. See how many scenes return. Can the director tell the cast what the theme or motif was/is? Does everyone agree? (it's okay if not everyone thinks that "Love" was the theme... in fact, that's the true test of art.. it means different things to different people even though we all just watched a scene about a pet burial.)

Try it again, but this time end the form after forty-five minutes. Keep adding time increments until the cast feels comfortable. The ultimate is for everyone to know when the show is over together.   M o r e on directing long-form improvisation later.

Coaching and Directing Long-form Improvisation

In Chicago, there is a definite distinction between the positions of coach and director. A coach usually is brought onto an existing team or ensemble to help them reach a stated artistic goal. His/her mission is to help the group discover themselves as a group entity. A director, on the other hand, usually fills a cast themselves in order to flesh out/perform a chosen show. Sometimes the cast has a vision and hires a director to help bring it to the stage and then the director is no longer required, whereas a coach is usually an on-going creative assistance.

Coaching an ensemble

The group comes first. You should be there to assist them in their chosen endeavor; whether it's on-going shows at a particular venue or sporadic performances in different locales. You're probably friends with the cast, but for the hour or two you will be rehearsing (and I do recommend at least two hours, but no more than three) you need to be a supervisor and in charge. Here are some tips for coaches:

Be punctual. Starting a rehearsal on time will help ensure that people arrive on time. If they believe that rehearsal "always" begins late, they will arrive later and later.

Let's be frank, sometimes these rehearsals will be right after a 9-to-5 job or late at night. Try to limit the food consumption; people tend to bring food and eat it during rehearsal which is distracting to everyone, not to mention the people who are still hungry!

The power of constructive criticism cannot be overemphasized. Improv comes from a very personal, internal place. Any criticism of someone's improv is sometimes misconstrued as too harsh, always find something good to like in anyone's performance.

Don't lie, but get into the habit of finding the good with the bad.

Give notes right after the show. As an improv show begins to fade from people's memories, their ability to learn from your notes fades as well. Keep your notes and use them at the beginning of your next rehearsal. Review what is needed and create/bring exercises that will specifically address the "problem areas".

You are not God. While you will be Scoutmaster and Den Mother all in one for a little bit, remember that you have much to learn from each performance and rehearsal as well. The moment either of these things become boring and rote to you is the time for you to take a vacation. Remember, that you can be wrong as well. Maybe you misheard something or missed something on stage. No big deal.. you're human.

Keep rehearsals interesting. Change up exercises and warm-ups. If you keep experimenting, you (and they) will keep learning.

DIRECTING LONGFORM IMPROVISATION

Second City teacher and director Michael Gellman once said that "a director is simply an educated audience of one" and he's right; it's a director's job to watch, observe, and then to give notes, advice and criticism with a wealth of experience and (one presumes) talent to back him/her up.   As stated earlier, you must have a director that is not a cast member. All of the suggestions for a coach apply doubly to a director. Assuming that the end result of a director's time with an ensemble is a show with an opening date, things in rehearsal will grow and evolve. create exercises and/or warm-ups that are specific to the form/show instead of just some random one.

Don't be afraid to be critical. You are directing a show, not coaching. Your primary concern should be the show and how it is created. Don't be a jerk about it, but criticism should be to the point and constructive. Give reasons for your direction/choices. ("We should edit like this because it helps the flow of the piece" , or "I'm cutting the monologues so the entire cast is better represented.") Have a clear vision of what you would like the end piece to look like, but be willing to adapt with the cast. That is, a clear vision will help you to articulate what you want, but if the cast doesn't adapt, you can't beat them into doing it "right", you too, must be able to adapt and evolve. Adapt to the stage. Use the full capabilities of your environment if your form permits it. Use the lighting, the trapdoors, the curtains. Don't use them gratuitously, but if they're there, why not? Examine your form. Is it fun to watch? Fun to perform? Does it allow enough freedom for the performers to play? How are the scenes? Are they allowed room to grow?

Timing! What is the length of your show? If you're charging money you should be giving your audience their monies worth (time-wise, at least). A full-length improv show should be at least an hour (give or take 5-10 minutes).

Scenic Exercises

Name: Two-from-a-Hat   What: Put everyone's name on a slip of paper and throw them all into a hat. Pull two names and have them do a two minute scene. Keep the used names out of the sort and do a round until everyone has gone. Mix them up and do it again, this time letting the scenes go even longer.   Why: Most ensembles, especially ones that have been around for a long time, tend to fall into the subconscious habit of only doing scenes with specific people. This exercise will help throw their scene partners into a random order.

Name: Three on A Match   What: Have two people do a scene. At the end of the scene, add another player to the scene and have all three do the same exact scene again as if the new player was in the original one. After this, rotate the players and do another two-person scene. Why: This will not only help with listening, it will help with creating three person scenes that aren't based on a "Us vs. Him" mentality (a common three-person scene pitfall.)

Name: Spin-off   What: Two people do a scene. At the end of the scene, two different people do a scene that is based in the world that the previous two players established. The scene could take place in a restaurant they mentioned or at one of the character's workplace. The trick is to not dwell on the previous scene, but exist in the same world. Why: This type of exercise aids in developing listening skills and in creating a shared world, things that will greatly aid a long-form piece.

Name: Directors Cut   What: Two people do a scene. The director/coach/whomever is in charge calls the end. After a very brief discussion of the scene, we continue the same exact scene from the last line. Let this scene go for a lonnng time; 7 to 10 minutes is a good length. Why: Any good scene should have the potential to be 20 minutes long. This exercise will help improvisers create more interesting, intelligent characters with the simple knowledge that they will be that character for longer than usual. The more emotion and depth they invest in a character will encourage them to treat it with respect.

Name: Story-into-scenes   What: A player, based on a suggestion, tells a story from his/her life. Two people then improvise a scene based a theme or emotion from the story. Repeating details from the story is not necessary or wanted. It's more important to find a theme and express it scenically. Why: This simple game focuses and sharpens the ability to discern a theme in any given source.

Name: Emotional Gift What: Two players take the stage. One will initiate the scene, while the other will react strongly with an emotion that has been secretly given to them by the instructor/ coach. The performers then switch (one initiates while the other responds). Why: to demonstrate how much more fun and rewarding a scene can be when strong emotions are attached to it. This exercise can be expanded to a large group.

ENSEMBLE EXERCISES

Name: Franchise   What: a more elaborate version of the exercise "Spin-off". Several scenes are created by using a first, "master" scene as a source. The "spin-off" scenes do not involve the characters from the first scene, but instead use the world they created to live in. We could see siblings, bosses, etc. based on the first two characters, but the scenes should not rely on them.   Why: Creating and exploring a world is a fun way to improvise and teaches how rewarding listening and connecting can be.

Name: Ménage   What: Two people improvise a "master" scene. A new player initiates a scene with one of the "master" scene characters, then a new player initiates a scene with the other character. Then both new characters do a scene and that becomes a new "master" scene for the other players to build on. Each scene should be a whole, interesting, relationship-based scene without referring or relying on the previous scenes.   Why: It reinforces the skill of creating scene that have a back-story without necessarily depending on that knowledge. It's like have an emergency $100 bill in your wallet... you may not need it, but it's good to know it's there.

Sketch shows

Sketch shows and improvisation have a strong relationship in that many people will attempt to translate a well-done improvised scene into scripted material. Obviously that formula works, as Chicago's venerable Second City theater has proven over the past 40 years. Using scenic (not long-form) improv, the Second City creates their sketch shows. This is an excellent tool for any improviser but actually, this is a hindrance to a long-form improv show. An improv show should be fireworks; graceful and powerful, not in spite of, but because of its fleeting and ephemeral nature. There's a reason that televised versions of fireworks and long-form improv never really hold up—it's difficult to capture the experience of actually being there for the magic. Your improv show should only have to shoulder the burden of being an improv show... if scripted material can be coaxed from it, then that's a great side effect, not an end goal. Focusing on great improv will produce great improv shows... forcing an improvised show to create show fodder will dilute your focus and your product. After an improv show, discussing what can be scripted out or reviewed a videotape of a show is a great idea as long as the players are not hindered by that process on stage.

Zen & the Art of Long-Form Improvisation

Zen is the ancient philosophy of "meditation in pursuit of an unmediated awareness of the processes of the world and the mind." The ultimate goal is to know oneself fully as well as one's place in the world. This is the Ultimate Enlightenment. By quieting the inner turmoil one can conquer external conflict with ease.

You've heard of the Zen axiom of "being in the moment." It is this state of mind, this calmness of Self, that creates a great improviser. The ability to accept and work with any given situation is a tenet of both Zen and long-form improvisation.   As I studied the philosophies of both Zen and the Asian martial arts I found many similar concepts and precepts. In fact, there were many similar exercises in their training classes. I regularly recommend the book "Zen and the Art of Archery" (as outdated as that book may seem) and the wonderful book "Hagakure: The Book of the Samurai" to my improvisation students.

Here are some quotes and ideas from various Zen and martial art sources and how they apply to the art of long-form improvisation:

> ## Knowing others is wisdom; knowing yourself is Enlightenment.
> ### - Lao-Tzu

Characters that know each other, have a shared past, have a greater emotional resonance with each other, have more fun. At the same time, knowing the past and thoughts and opinions of the character we're playing is one of the best things we can do onstage.

Nothing is impossible to a willing mind.
- Books of the Han Dynasty

This is the very heart of "Yes, and..." Accept gleefully the improvised concepts of your reality and use it to it's full extent. Take the time to invest in it both with your mind and your environment.

The angry man will defeat himself in battle as well as in life.
- Samurai maxim

It's good to be emotional in your scene work, but anger is the toughest one to play. Strong emotions, particularly anger, should never interfere with your ability to have a relationship with your scene partner.

To know and to act are one and the same
- Samurai maxim

(I take this one two ways.) Since we know ourselves (our characters) so well, we should be able to exist within a scene without revealing (relying on) that it is improvised. That is, the acting is strong because we know and act as one. Another way to take this maxim is that since we are these characters so fully, why shouldn't the environment be as fully realized? Know the place the scene occurs in and use it to its fullest.

Technical knowledge is not enough. One must transcend techniques so that the art becomes an artless art, growing out of the unconscious.
- Daisetsu Suzuki

Just as in the martial arts, where one learns set responses to certain actions (taking a fall, rolling with a punch, responding to different holds, etc.), in long-form improvisation we can learn certain techniques (like the great ones found in first part of this book) so that they become second nature and great improv "grows out of the unconscious."

When you expect something, when you aim at something, right there you dilute your energy; you split your energy, you split your attention and it becomes more than a place of yin and yang. You do not only divide, but you create the problem. - Taizon Maezumi

Don't enter/begin a scene with expectations of where it should go. If you enter with a plot or a plan you will distract yourself from truly hearing your scene partner and therefore, be unable to respond with honest emotion.

If you cannot find the truth right where you are, where else do you expect to find it?
- Dogen Zenji

Sometimes improvisers will create a situation where the scene would be more interesting someplace else! In the future, the place they're going, anywhere but where they are at that very moment. Stop. Relax. The scene is right there. Right there, between the two people on stage. You don't have to go anywhere unless you wish to... the scene is there.

Empty your mind, be formless. Shapeless, like water. If you put water into a cup, it becomes the cup. You put water into a bottle and it becomes the bottle. You put it in a teapot it becomes the teapot. Now, water can flow or it can crash. Be water my friend.
-Bruce Lee

Don't be trapped by your own expectations of what should happen; let your self flow and adapt to everything. Without prejudice, without assuming, you will find scene work easier and more fun as you and your scene partner evolve and adapt to, and with, each other.

When you seek it, you cannot find it.
- J. Hyams

In comedy there's very little worse than someone desperately trying to be funny. Don't look to be funny. Look to do great scene work and concentrate on creating the whole and the "Funny" will find you.

The following essays are from my on-line blog. I hope they are instrumental to you.

The Rape of Improv

Words are powerful and in no other medium is this as evident as in long-form improvisation. The words we speak are so much more powerful and honest because we don't have time to consider and ponder. When we are improvising well and from our heart that's when our words spring from our ID, our hearts, or even our souls. We should wear our hearts, if not our motivations all the time, on our sleeves. Are there topics that are taboo to us? Should certain words or thoughts be forbidden for exploration on stage? I don't think so and yet I think we should be careful as to our motivations in bringing certain subjects up on stage. We can (and should) be free to say what we want if we aren't doing it for a "free" laugh or simply for shock value. I recently had a class and the subject of rape came up during the course of a rehearsal. I won't get into the details, but a female character was repeatedly told she had been raped and even had the nickname "Rapey" in the police department she worked in. In other scenes she was told to get over it and eventually she pulled her gun and killed people. At the end of the Harold, the class wasn't very happy. They all felt uncomfortable with what had happened and so did I. To tell you the truth, the technical aspects of the Harold were well done and the gameplay was strong, but it was the subject matter that made everyone feel upset. We talked about it and we did our best to figure out what went wrong where. I couldn't put my finger on it or clearly define how best to deal with it. I didn't want to say "don't do" that sort of scene, but obviously, we had hit a bump in the road. Later that night, I watched a 12:30am presentation of "Fat and Skinny" featuring Danny Mora and Andy St. Clair with special guest star Molly Erdman. We know from the first scene that a college basketball coach eventually gets fired from her job because her players are convicted for rape. The show then moved between two scenes; a coach with her two basketball players and a stripper with the same players. This show was smart and hilarious. What was the difference? Choice and initiation. In the late night show, the female player initiated the move to be the "victim", the "stripper" (turns out she works at Home Depot as a vinyl siding stripper). As she "parties" with the two players it was the female character that initiated each game move of more and more hazardous interaction (drinking more beer, wrestling.) The male characters swiftly agreed, but never physically intimidated or threatened their fellow player. A strong "respect of space" was used. Even when the female character laid down on the floor, the male players chose to edit back to the coach scene. In the coach scenes, the power position was with the female character that berated the males and used her status to good effect. Rape is definitely about power and in the late show we saw how a strong player can keep the power and use it to control our (the audience) perceptions. Never once was the female stripper in danger (even though we know that this scene is in the past and she does indeed get raped) on stage. The control of the scene was in her hands, both as character and player. In the class, the role of victim was laid onto a female player and reinforced by the other players.

Del Close once said in class, "There's no damn justice in the world, why not create some on stage?" The philosophy of "yes, and" isn't a rule that should hamper you or make you, well, dumb. It's a basic tenet that our characters live in a shared universe with a set structure of physics. If someone calls you "retarded" it doesn't mean your character is necessarily a mentally handicapped person. If someone says it's freezing out it doesn't necessarily mean that your character is instantly cold. You can have differences of opinion. Your character can have beliefs and ideas of their own without violating "yes, and." My point is that in improv no one can make you/your character a victim without your permission. Be strong and fight back and use your wits to create an interesting scene. Just shouting "no" won't help, but adding some emotion and power will always help. Conversely, I have found that most scenes are present and good within four lines… profanity, racism, words for shock value are the first refuge of the incompetent improviser. Certainly, those things can and should be part of our lexicon but in their place and context, not thrown out for a "free" laugh. If that's all you got, you're not fun to watch.   I hope no one thinks I'm coming down on my students. My amazement is from all this happening on the same day. Watching both, I could feel myself learning and processing what I had learned. I have already shared these things with the class and we have one more session. I frequently tell students, and it never felt more clear than this week, that the main thing separating them from their teachers, from their favorite performers, is time. Time, experience, showing up and making so many mistakes that you learn from them and wish to share those mistakes with others so that they may avoid the same path.   We're all learning together.

Cashing In

One of the major questions improvisers get is "how do you make any money"? There are few and far between shows that compensate their performers (with pride, the cast and crew of Whirled News Tonight gets a check every month) while most players across Chicago must make do with the applause and laughter from a paying crowd.

The greatest supplement to an actor's income is the much beloved, and much detested, corporate gig. ALL major theaters have a corporate division. Sometimes it means selling special shows or nights to large corporations (the show might be at a special time, but the content is unaltered. The house is buy-out.) Sometimes it means a specially created show for a client. Like, if there's a new product to sell, a company might hire a troupe to create a special show for their sales people to help explain (or even to celebrate) the new item.   Now, the absolute BEST corporate gig is the special event show. These shows usually involve travel and a giant show with many presentations by the corporation's executives with sketches or games in-between the speeches. These usually pay the best.   People always want in on these jobs and it's both really hard and really easy to get into. Second City, ComedySportz and iO all have divisions that do/sell all of the above corporate work. There are also very successful independent companies doing very lucrative jobs that have strong ties to the improv world. Sometimes they have auditions and sometimes they just ask you if you're available.   Besides special skills like being able to use an ear-prompter, teleprompter or one of those things we all say we can do on the bottom of our resumes, some of the most important skills or features a corporate performer has are quite simple: punctuality   able to work as a team   always says "YES, let's do it" instead of creating problems   learns their lines fast, and is able to cope with many changes   has a suit   polite and friendly when with clients   knows the boundaries and ethics of friendly business interaction   Getting to travel with other improv people is lots of fun. Getting to do shows or classes for people who might never see improv is very rewarding as well. Being part of the "fun part" of a giant presentation is rewarding as well. Of course, getting paid well (as opposed to being a receptionist for 12 an hour (which I was not too long ago) is an amazing reward and always us to continue to create our art.   Bottom line is that you should do good work. Let the people who book these sort of jobs know that you're available and if you have any special skills they should use. A headshot, resume, and nice cover letter go a long way. Be available to them as well; if you have one of those jobs where you can't take days off you can't do this sort of work usually.   Have a good reputation. By that I mean that you shouldn't be a jerk. Treat your fellow cast members and teammates as working professionals. Don't get dragged down into gossip and back-biting. If someone asks someone else about you they should be able to say, "Oh, s/he's great!" without adding the dreaded "… exxcepptt…."

Shtick in a Box

There is no doubt that the advent of YouTube and online comedy content has affected television comedy. How it is purchased, written, edited, etc… all of it has been drastically affected by the short, straight-to-the-point, accessible, DIY videos. Corporate America has had a very tough time catching up to, much less competing with, a group of five funny people with PCs and a camera. Comedy festivals are filled with networks and producers looking for the next Lonely Island (which, of course, they all initially ignored), the next big online thing. Just like the 80s explosion of cable channels, this online explosion of "supply" has suddenly created a demand. More and more corporate sponsored "channels" need content and they're willing to pay for it, too.

But the question for us is should it affect what we do onstage? Quicker? More accessible? Do we acquiesce to what we think an audience wants? I don't think so. If we're trying to bring people out of their homes and into a theater we need to strive for something different. The Internet, movies, cable, NetFlix… those are our competitors! We can't beat them for ease-of-use or simplicity. We should try to do better than those things… what can we do better? What can we offer that they cannot?   We're live. The excitement of being in the same room of performers is something we should capitalize on. We have the incredible ability to present longer, more human characters AND the wonderful opportunity to deal with abstract, deep ideas. We have to have the courage to do those things. We have to give ourselves the permission to do those things. We have to have the balls to speak truth to power, to cut deep and hard. Online content is changing television and movie comedy, but it shouldn't change us. It should challenge us to do better. And that's not just a challenge to performers. It's a challenge to producers. Don't think people will come to see what they can see at home. Sure, they will in the short-term, but what does your building offer that no one does? THAT'S what brings people in.

Topical Paradise

"Sir, what exactly would you like to see on stage tonight?" – Del Close, in response to the suggestion of "assassination", weeks after the death of RFK.*

After national tragedies, what is the responsibility of the improviser? As performers, are we simply on-stage to entertain or are our duties broader than that? I think that part of that decision depends on what doorway a paying customer is entering through. Does the door open into a comedy club or to a theater? What are they paying to see? A comedy show, or a performance art? Which is it? To jarringly bring up a tragedy to seem topical does a disservice both to the audience and to the "nothing scripted" philosophy of improvisation. The show "Whirled News Tonight" certainly touches on sensitive topics; that's part of the reason the show was created. The audience chooses articles and places them on stage; the performers randomly pull from that collection. There are two "blinds", as it were. Frequently, the audience decides to not post any touchy subjects even if they were the headlining stories. We don't decide to avoid topics or subjects and frequently we find connections to the major stories of the day even if the articles don't (seemingly) refer to them. We have found that you can make fun of any situation. Everything is fodder for comedy, except for certain people. You cannot and should not make fun of the victims of anything. It goes to the idea that comedy should attack the strong and powerful. Watching a feeble person desperately attempt to lift a cup won't be as funny as a Hercules falling down a flight of stairs (right there. That makes me laugh.. a greased up Arnold Schwarzenegger from "Hercules Goes Bananas" falling down a flight of stairs…) The laws, the government, the social structures, the companies that created the dire situation or failed to act; those are our targets. The victims are not fodder for comedy.   I recently reprimanded a student for his (and it's always a "HE") frequent use of the word "faggot." Then we all went downstairs for the Deep Schwa show and that word was used quite a bit to the delight of the audience. But here's the rub; it wasn't the word that was getting the laughs/reactions; it was the in-character emotional reaction to the word. The character being addressed was hurt, and then angry, by the use of the word.   I have no trouble with any words used on stage as long as they are honest words. A word, such as "bitch", "faggot", "Chink", any profane pejorative, shouldn't be your punch line. As improvisers, words are our currency and we should be miserly with what we have amassed. If we decide to use a "risky" word it should be for a reason beyond shock-value. It should be a conscious decision.   The greatest comedies have been satires. The greatest satires have been smart and literate. Let us strive to be great.

*- possibly, most likely apocryphal.

Ten Easy Ways to Be a Better Improviser (in no particular order)

Listen. No, really. Really listen to what someone else says on stage before you react. If this means slowing down your reaction time, do so. It's not a race. Respond to what they're really saying.

Wipe the slate clean. Watch a show as if you've never seen improv before. The reason most people start doing long-form is because of a particular show and then over the years, and after watching hundreds of shows we all become jaded. Wipe the slate clean and watch all it anew. Try to recapture what drew you to the art in the first place.

Shut up. Make a personal moratorium on gossip and back-biting. Not a resolution (those rarely last) but a 1 month hiatus from a destructive habit that has a tendency to spill onto stage.

Know thyself. You know what you always do. Stop that. If you're always a nerdy character change that. If you're always a foreigner, stop that. Change starts with you (you know, like the Man in the Mirror); surprise your fellow performers by playing out of "character" for yourself. (this also goes for habits like: always initiating, being very verbose, singing, et al.)

Transformation. Change what you usually wear onstage. If you don't already; try wearing a suit for your show. Or try wearing new shoes. It will not only change how you move, but how an audience perceives you even before you do anything.

Go see a show. Go see theater outside of the world of improv and sketch. Anything. Observe how that group uses their space, dresses, and presents their craft. It will either inform and educate or inspire you do the same or better.

Make a plan. Plan out what your goals are and what you'd like to have done by the end of the year. Produce your first improv show? Direct an sketch show? Take another class? Improvisation as a lifestyle only goes so far; make a list and put it somewhere where you can see it.

Watch a rehearsal. Ask a team you admire if you could watch their rehearsal. You'll learn a lot. Don't take notes, don't ask questions (during the session) and remember that things said and done are private. Make sure that everyone is aware and okay with you attending.

Write it down. Take one scene from your last class/rehearsal/show and script it out. Give a copy to everyone involved in it. Iron it out. Make sure to date it.

Before your show, watch the previous teams/shows. Don't repeat what they've done in style, tone or presentation. Throw the audience a change-up; be different in energy, volume and ideas.

It's a Big World. Let's all agree to have a four week hiatus from any roommate, first date/pick-up, job interview, Dr./Patient scenes.

Cast vs. Team

There are three kinds of improv ensembles; teams, casts and pick-ups. Casts are created in order to follow the form or show premise/concept. The function will follow the form. Pick-ups are randomly chosen or haphazardly put together groups of people to do a show (usually just one performance.) For now, let's focus on "teams."   What makes a great improv team?   A general consensus or group agreement as to the style of the team.   Group dedication to the process (rehearsals, performances, notes, et al.)   An equally dedicated coach (someone who gives strong constructive notes, conducts rehearsals and attends the shows, and usually, keeps the peace.)   It's more difficult for newer teams to achieve the first two; some performers are still finding their own "voice" on stage, much less able to find a group mind. In the beginning, when players and shows are new, it's imperative for rehearsals to be productive meetings.   Time is Money.   When a team starts meeting and begins to rehearse, there's money involved. Here in Chicago the average honorarium is $5 per player per rehearsal to the coach. Usually, a room is rented at a Park District building or behind/above a bar somewhere. So a typical rehearsal might end up costing a player anywhere from $5 to $10 a week. That's not cheap.. especially if you're relatively new to Chicago and you still have a jay-oh-bee (as opposed to a career or where you don't have to punch-in or have someone sign your card). So, rehearsals=time+money. If you're late, don't show up, disrupt, don't listen, argue, etc. during rehearsal you're wasting everyone's time and money and you're a jerk.   If you're on a team and you notice that Person A usually does all the organizing and arranging of space and personnel, offer to help out. Maybe for the next month, you'll do it. Lighten the load… no one should have to feel that they're responsible for the entire rehearsal.   No! then Go! Then TELL!   If a fellow player makes you uncomfortable and it's disrupting your ability to improvise, then you should tell your coach in private. If your coach is the perpetrator, then you should tell whomever is in charge of your organization (the head of a training center, someone on the "board", etc…). If you're uncomfortable with that, try consulting with someone you trust who's been around a while at that organization. Don't tell rumors, don't spread gossip… tell them the truth and facts of what's happening with you and your group.

Some Guidelines for Players: Don't be late for shows or rehearsals. Don't miss rehearsals and then show up for the shows. Consult with the coach to see if you should watch.   Take the note.   Stay for notes after your show. Listen to them.   What works on stage works off stage as well; Listen to what people say, "yes, and…" don't argue.   Respect your fellow players and your coach. Even if you don't, act like you do.   Communicate! Let people know your opinions and your schedule, but don't hold them hostage to either. Some Guidelines & Advice for Coaches: Don't be late for shows or rehearsals.   Realize that coaching is actually two jobs; rehearsals and shows. If you can't do both, you're not doing the job.

Your notes should never be longer than the show.   Notes are constructive criticism from an outside eye; it's not simply a rehash of what happened or a bitch-out session. Players, regardless of the show, should feel better after notes.   Doing the lights for your team can only help. Lights up & down is boring; use the spots, slow fade, etc.. it will make the show more theatrical and you (should) know the team better than anyone else.

Consider the players under your tutelage your students, treat them accordingly.   Don't have favorites, don't have unfavorites.

Bitch Fest

I am profane. Not only do I cuss, I curse, I swear, I use up a lot of expletives. People who have done a scripted show with me know that when it's late, and I'm tired, and we're behind schedule, you get to hear a lot of swear words. Even as I teach, I tend to lapse into profanity, so obviously, I'm not adverse to hearing those words on stage. In fact, I think it usually adds an air of realism to what is supposed to be "real". Imagine the Sopranos with no profanity. It wouldn't be "real." (One of my favorite Mr. Show sketches was the spoof of the movie Goodfellas, called "Pallies". They show the edited-for-television version with dubbed in words for the curses; "Mother-father!" and my favorite (almost non-sequitor) "Chinese Dentist!") Sit-coms have increasingly used the word "bitch" as a punch line. Usually, a character will be yelled at or shown up in some fashion and then is left alone. A beat goes by and then the character will mutter, "bitch." And then a voice from off-camera says, "I heard that!" I have a great problem with the word "bitch." "Bitch" has become a punch line, a joke. It's probably trickle down desensitization from stand-up comedy. Usually, it's a male using it. Surprise! The word gets handled like a war hammer, it gets swung around, smashing everything in its path with the wielder hoping it gets a laugh somewhere. But all the blame cannot be laid on the person who says it. We have to look at the reactions we give that word and all words in improvisation. Who are we to each other on-stage? What's our relationship? Mother/son, husband/wife, girlfriend/boyfriend, coworkers, etc? That will affect both the words we choose and how we react to an outré profanity.

Regardless of the relationship, most women I know would not let me calling them a "bitch" just flow over them. They would react and react strongly and I think that's important. I'm willing to bet that if most men called their mother, girlfriend, wife, co-worker, a "bitch" it would change the tenor of their conversation.   Don't use profanity as a punch line. You're smarter than that. WE'RE smarter than that.   Don't let your "son", "husband", "boyfriend", "co-worker" get away with using certain types of profanity in your presence. Be real. React! React with emotion.   Thanks for listening to me bitch.

(note there was no comma in that sentence)

Some Quick Reminders & Tips

It is improvising. Not impro, not bits, not make em ups, not "improvs".

You're an improviser. If you're any good, you're an actor who is able to do a show without a script. If you're a comedian, great. I hope you can act. Otherwise, you're quickly the most annoying guy at the party.

Being dumb is not excusable. If you feel, if you know that an area of your knowledge is somehow less than what you're comfortable with, then fix it. Go to the library. Buy a used book. Ask someone who knows.

Being smart doesn't automatically make you a great improviser. Most of the great improvisers have been very intelligent, but not every great intellect is a great improviser. Sometimes the brains get in the way of the heart. "Spock! You're half human, remember!"

Love and learn. Love to learn new things and people. Learn to love those people and the things you cannot change.

Keep moving and evolving. Be like a Shark… keep moving. Welcome, promote, encourage positive change.

Jay Sandrich (look him up in IMDB, or you know, not) once told me, "Watch everything. Learn to know what you love and what you hate, but WHY you love something and WHY you hate something… it's not enough to love or hate something; you have to know why."

Don't strive to be the "next" Anyone. Take what they've done and build on it. Create your own you. "If I have seen further than others it is because I have stood on the shoulders of giants." – Isaac Newton

Getting drunk is not a good way to make friends or "bond". Relaxing and having an actual conversation with someone is, and no one has ever gone UP in someone's estimation by getting wasted.

The very simple rules of "yes, and", "arguing is boring", "stop shouting", "don't deny", etc., also apply to your sketch show.

You improvise scenes. Not sketches or skits.   A sketch is something that will be elaborated on later and in more detail.   A skit is a short humorous or dramatic work, usually written.

Girls, there are guys in improv who are dicks; don't date them.   Guys, don't be the dick that girls warn other girls about.

If you get high more than three times a week, you're getting high too much. Lay off the pot, kids.

There is more creativity in the improv community than any other place in the world. What the improv community lacks is follow-through. Write that script and actually finish it. Rent space and produce that great improv show.

Use your improv poster to tell me how your show is unique from the 100 other improv shows/teams in the city.   Get healthier.   Stop quoting tv shows. On or offstage.

Don't be afraid to get a real job. Despite all the literature to the contrary, being a starving artist really fucking sucks. No one out of college, regardless of age, should be eating Ramen noodles.

Treat rehearsals like you treat shows; be punctual, schedule accordingly, listen and support.

Your coach/teacher/director is not god. Question a note or critique. Then shut up. It's not debate club.   Your coach/teacher/director is not sacrosanct. No matter who they are they have a boss. If something unprofessional happens, if something crosses the line, report it.

Ask yourself why you're doing improv. Why are you taking those classes and going to rehearsals and watching shows and doing shows? To what end? To be on SNL? To get on a House Team? To be on Mainstage? To get on TV? To be in the movies? If the answer is yes, then your aim is off. Of course, those things do happen to very talented and lucky people. But you need to concentrate on the more immediate goal; being a great improviser. First do that. And

Sometimes,

once in a while,

shut up about improv.

Afterword

I hope that this book proves useful to you in your work with long-form improvisation. It's a fascinating art form that continues to evolve and mutate. I believe the trend is towards longer and longer shows with smaller and smaller casts (in numbers, not height) which allows for more intimate emotions and intense performances. Being in and part of the moment on stage is how a true artist expresses his or her self onstage. It's not jokes or quickness of wit, but the creation of a world of emotion and ideas that will last beyond the performance and help improv become a true art form.   Thank you.